The Complete System for Building Profitable Luxury Theme Pages

A COMPLETE GUIDE
Get started creating your luxury theme page
and find out how to achieve success.

'IT ALWAYS SEEMS IMPOSSIBLE UNTIL IT'S DONE.'

NELSON MANDELA

Discipline > Motivation

Content

Chapter 1:
The Luxury Theme
Page Opportunity

 What does this faceless business model entail?

Why Luxury Theme Pages Are a Goldmine

In today's digital landscape, luxury theme pages represent a lucrative yet underutilized opportunities in social media. While countless creators struggle to monetize their content, luxury theme pages tap into a unique market to make them profitable. Let me show you why.

Luxury theme pages capitalize on a fundamental human desire: aspiration. Your audience isn't just scrolling through pretty pictures – they're investing time in their future vision of success. This psychological connection creates an unprecedented level of engagement that standard theme pages simply cannot match. When followers engage with luxury content, they're not just liking photos; they're affirming their own goals and dreams.

What makes Luxury Theme Pages Valuable?

Luxury pages can be monetized through various channels simultaneously:
- Affiliate marketing
- Mentoring
- VIP membership programs
- Exclusive resources
- Digital products and courses

WHY IS IT THE PERFECT TIME?
- AI and automation make content creation more efficient
- New monetization tools are constantly emerging
- We are in an attention economy

Luxury pages are also *faceless*

Faceless marketing is a strategic approach to building an online presence and generating income without revealing your physical identity. This method focuses on crafting a powerful brand identity through words, visuals, and a unique persona, rather than relying on a visible face.

Faceless marketing represents an exciting opportunity to build a thriving online business without the limitations of a traditional personal brand. With the right mindset and execution, you'll be well on your way to achieving the financial freedom you desire.

This e-book will guide you through the process of building your own personal and faceless brand in the luxury theme page niche on Instagram, and leveraging it to create a stream of income through the sale of digital products.

The key to faceless marketing lies in developing a strong, cohesive brand that captivates your audience and establishes your expertise, even in the absence of a visible face. By mastering this approach, you'll be empowered to achieve financial freedom and independence.

Throughout this comprehensive guide, you'll learn the strategies and techniques necessary to build a successful faceless brand, including:
- Establishing a consistent, visually appealing brand identity across all your online touchpoints
- Crafting a compelling personal narrative and storytelling approach to connect with your audience
- Leveraging value-driven content to attract and retain a loyal community
- Strategizing the creation and promotion of your digital product offerings
- Automating your marketing and sales processes for sustainable growth

There are also many perks to making your business faceless:

More Privacy: You don't have to worry about being recognized in public or having your identity exposed.

Less Pressure: Without your face showing, you don't have to worry as much about looking perfect all the time. Your main focus is your content and the value you provide to your audience.

Time Flexibility: You can pre-schedule posts and take time off when needed without disrupting your brand's flow.

Creativity Freedom: You're able to fully create and showcase your skills without feeling the pressure of being judged.

Keeps The Professionalism: If you are a professional and don't want to be discovered by co-workers or business partners, this a great way.

Are you ready to embark on this transformative journey and unlock your full potential as an entrepreneur?
This e-book is your roadmap to success.

Chapter 2: Building The Foundation

 Where do we start?

What does your ideal customer look like?

Let's get into the mind of your **ideal customer**, here's your framework:

1. Core Demographics
Age, Gender, Location, Occupation, Income level

2. Psychological Profile
Primary goals and ambitions, Biggest fears and frustrations, Daily challenges, Dreams and aspirations, Values and beliefs, What keeps them up at night?

3. Lifestyle Characteristics
Hobbies and interests, Brands they love, Social media habits, Where they spend their time online, How they consume content, Shopping behaviors, Investment in personal development

4. Their Journey
Where are they now?, Where do they want to be?, What's stopping them?, What solutions are they seeking?, How can you help them?

Think about it!

Your Ideal Client

Create a comprehensive profile of your ideal client, it's essential to include various aspects such as demographics, psychographics and goals. This will help you understand their challenges, desires, and preferences, enabling you to serve them more effectively.

_____
_____
_____
_____
_____
_____
_____
_____
_____
_____
_____
_____
_____
_____
_____
_____
_____
_____
_____
_____
_____
_____

Identify Pain Points and Desires

Make a list of the most common pain points and desires your ideal client experiences. Brainstorm solutions and offerings that address these challenges and fulfill their aspirations. Consider how you can position your products or services as the ultimate solution to their problems.

_____

_____

_____

_____

_____

_____

_____

_____

_____

_____

_____

_____

_____

_____

_____

_____

_____

_____

_____

_____

_____

_____

Once you understand your detailed customer profile, use it as a filter for everything you do:

Content Creation

Would your dream customer find this valuable?
Does it speak to their specific goals and challenges?
Is it presented in a way they prefer to consume content?

Visual Aesthetics

Does your page design appeal to their taste level?
Are you featuring brands and experiences they aspire to?
Does your content quality match their expectations?

Communication Style

Are you using language that resonates with them?
Do your captions address their specific interests?
Are you posting at times when they're most active?

Product Development

What specific problems can you solve for them?
What format would they prefer for educational content?
What price point matches their investment capability?

Remember, your dream customer profile isn't static. You'll refine and adjust this profile as you interact with your audience and gather **feedback**. The key is starting with a clear, specific vision of who you're serving and letting that guide your strategy.

Your Profile

Your Instagram profile serves as your digital face in the faceless page space – it must exude premium quality from the first glance.

Start with your username: choose something memorable that reflects luxury while remaining professional. Avoid underscores or numbers as much as possible unless absolutely necessary. Your display name should include a key luxury keyword that helps with discoverability.

The bio section becomes your elevator pitch. In the luxury niche, less is more. Structure your bio in three parts:
- A clear value proposition (what your page offers)
- Credibility markers (key achievements or focus areas)
- A compelling call-to-action

Example of an optimized luxury page bio:

Curating Exceptional Luxury Lifestyle
Featured in Robb Report & Luxe Digital
↓ Exclusive Luxury Insights
[Link to premium offering]

Optimizing your profile

Now, we are focused on luxury theme pages here, so we are going to zero in on utilizing Instagram as our avenue for growth and development. As it is a top performing platform when it comes to building your brand and growing through marketing.
Let's focus on how you can optimize your theme page:

Name the Page

When naming your luxury page, the goal is to clearly communicate your offering to your target audience. Consider incorporating your niche or theme, but avoid overly narrow or restrictive names that may limit your future business growth. Some tips:

- You don't necessarily need to include the word "luxury" in your page name

- Make it unique and have a good ring to it

- Choose a name that can adapt as your business evolves

- Make sure it reflects the content you wish to post

- If unsure, always use an AI like ChatGPT to help give you ideas

Optimize the Bio

Your Instagram bio is the first impression visitors get when viewing your luxury page. Optimize it to quickly communicate your value proposition and encourage engagement.

Key elements to include:

- A catchy, descriptive one-liner about your brand
- Clarification of your niche or product category
- Explanation of who you help and how you help them
- A clear call-to-action (e.g., drive traffic to your digital products)
- Strategic use of keywords for improved searchability (SEO)

Optional Bio Additions:

1. First Line: A snippet about your personal journey or transformation

Example

1. Second Line: Showcase any relevant accomplishments or authority-building credentials
2. Third Line: A powerful call-to-action

Finding Your Unique Point of Difference (POD)

Your POD is what sets your faceless brand apart and makes it more unique, valuable, interesting, inspiring, motivating, or entertaining than your competitors.

Use this template to define your POD:

"I am a [your niche] who specifically focuses on [what you do/who you do it for] through [the type of value you provide]."

By clearly articulating your POD, you can craft a compelling brand identity that resonates with your target audience and helps you stand out in the market.

Account Preparation

The email you use for your Instagram registration should be an aged account with existing activity in the inbox. Avoid using a brand-new email, as this can signal to Instagram that your account is potentially bot-driven. Ensure you have enabled all available security measures, such as two-factor authentication, to further demonstrate the authenticity of your account.

SECURITY SETTINGS

When setting up your Instagram account, populate it with as much security information as possible. This includes adding your personal details, profile picture, and bio. Bots typically lack these comprehensive security measures, so this step will help differentiate your account as a genuine human-operated profile.

ACCOUNT WARM-UP

Rather than immediately posting content, take the time to gradually warm up your account. Begin by searching for and engaging with relevant accounts in your chosen niche. Like 5-10 posts every hour, but avoid excessive commenting, as this can be interpreted as bot-like behavior. This warm-up period should last 24-72 hours before you start posting your own content.

TIMING YOUR FIRST POST

For the best results, aim to make your first post 48-72 hours after creating the account. This timing allows Instagram's systems to recognize your account as a genuine human-operated profile, rather than a bot-like entity.

By meticulously following these steps, you can establish a faceless Instagram presence that is perceived as authentic and organic by the platform.

Chapter 3
Faceless Content Strategy & Creation

How to start creating content using proven
concepts and strategies

Market Research

ANALYZE YOUR COMPETITORS
Identify the top-performing luxury-themed Instagram pages.
Examine their content, posting frequency, engagement, and which posts resonate with their audience.
Pay attention to the visual aesthetics, captions, and overall brand identity they've cultivated.
Take note of any gaps or areas where the page seems to fall and where you could potentially optimize in your own page.

IMMERSE YOURSELF IN LUXURY CONTENT
- Regularly consume content from leading luxury pages.
- Pay close attention to the visual styles, techniques, and themes that are prevalent in the luxury space.
- Analyze how these creators captivate their audience and inspire them to engage with the content.
- Identify opportunities to adapt and personalize these proven approaches to align with your unique brand identity.

You can use Social Media Competitive Analysis to streamline your market research on your competitors pages. You can also use a tool like Instagrammer to get fast analytics on your competitors

LEVERAGE SOCIAL ANALYTICS TOOLS

- Use tools to monitor relevant hashtags, keywords, and mentions related to your luxury niche.
- Analyze the sentiment, engagement, and trending topics surrounding luxury content.
- Gain insights into the content that your target audience is actively seeking, discussing, and sharing.
- Identify emerging luxury trends and content formats that you can incorporate into your own strategy.

By thoroughly researching your target market, analyzing your competition, and immersing yourself in the luxury content landscape, you'll be equipped to create a cohesive, visually stunning, and highly engaging Instagram presence that resonates with your desired audience. On the next page we will go through the content pillars essential for all your posts

Visual consistency becomes paramount in the luxury space, it's essentially your page's personality. Luxury pages must create their character through a sophisticated and consistent aesthetic. This means developing a signature visual style that could cause a viewer to stop scrolling. Think of your page as a digital magazine, where every post must meet the highest standards of visual excellence.

IDENTITY

Your identity encompasses everything from your profile image to the fonts and color schemes you utilize in your content. For luxury theme pages, maintaining a cohesive visual identity is crucial, as it enhances memorability and recognition among your audience. High-quality visuals that reflect elegance and smoothness can significantly elevate your page's aesthetic

CONSISTENCY

Consistency is key in branding. Ensure that your visual identity, content, and tone of voice are uniform across all posts. This includes adhering to a regular posting schedule to keep your audience engaged. The importance of this pillar cannot be overstated as inconsistency may negatively affect the algorithms output on your posts

Content Pillars

TONE OF VOICE

Your tone of voice reflects how you communicate with your audience through both written and spoken words. It encompasses the use of graphics, emojis, motivational quotes, and even calls to action. For luxury pages, both a visually appealing and articulate tone are necessary, as it grabs attention and gives an astounding feeling to your viewers.

ENGAGEMENT

To cultivate a robust community around your luxury page, regular engagement with your followers is essential. This can involve responding to comments and messages promptly or creating interactive polls and questions for your audience to connect with you and each other. Get creative, put yourself in your audiences shoes and engage accordingly.

How to source quality clips

The foundation of a good luxury theme page lies in your ability to source and share high-quality content. This section will reveal the strategies and sources used by other luxury pages to maintain premium content.

Luxurious instagram pages represent your first tier of content sources. Following and monitoring these sources provides you with high-quality content. However, the key is to curate and present this content in a unique way that adds value beyond simple reposting. A simple Instagram search for "luxury houses" luxury decor, luxury dining are various search names to find high quality videos to download from Instagram. We download them using Snapinsta.

Stock footage platforms have extensive libraries of luxury content. This method is not often used as the luxury clips are high quality but not as impactful as other methods. Most luxury pages source clips by purchasing clip packs from other creators or sourcing clips themselves on Instagram.

How to select the best quality clips

Once you have acquired the luxury clips the next step is to utilize them properly.

It is best to post clips on Instagram at 1080p with 30fps. Ensure to select cliips that are sharp and show clear details. The higher quality the video looks the better it will do in the algorithm. Choose an aesthetic theme for your videos to stand out. Examples would be a dark aesthetic or showcasing a specific car as the theme like a BMW or Porsche. Make sure that if you get a clip directly from another creator to give credit in your caption.

TO ENHANCE VIDEO QUALITY THE FOLLOWING
SOFTWARES CAN BE USED:
POWERDIRECTOR
TOPAZ VIDEO AI
AVCLABS VIDEO ENHANCER AI
HITPAW VIDEO ENHANCER
PIXOP
GDFLAB PIKAVUE

Remember, in the luxury space, quality isn't just about high resolution or perfect lighting, it's about creating an aspirational experience that is congruent with the luxury lifestyle.

Creating Viral Luxury Reels

Instagram Reels are the primary drivers of growth in the luxury niche. The key to viral luxury reels lies in understanding what works

Hooks are definitely things that work. Here are a few::
- "The only way to..." (exclusivity angle)
- "What they don't tell you about..." (insider information)
- "How the 1% actually..." (wealth insights)
- "Rare glimpse inside..." (exclusive access)
Use these as guides when making your hooks. In a later chapter we will dive into even more hook examples for you to use and highlight its importance

What to post:

Luxury lifestyle clips
Luxury cars
Money videos
Luxury interiors
Luxury properties
Beautiful sceneries
Ship clips
Plane clips
Luxury watchhes

This is short form content, meaning we don't want clips to be too long. Ideally we want 6 -11 seconds of video length . Your aspect ratio must be 9:16 vertical format to make sure your video perfectly fits on Instagram reels. Try to show your best clip within the first 3 seconds.

Captions

Your caption is a crucial element that shouldn't be overlooked. It should begin with a strong hook that grabs people's attention and encourages them to read the full caption.

For longer captions, it's important to break up the text into shorter, more digestible sentences or paragraphs. This makes it easier for your audience to focus and engage with the content.

Use emojis sparingly - don't overdo it. But a strategic use of emojis can help make your caption more visually appealing and engaging.

If your caption is captivating, lengthy (with proper spacing), and well-crafted, it can actually boost the performance of your reel, especially if it's a short 5-7 second clip. This will increase watch time and can lead to your content being shown to more people.

Remember to include all the essential elements in your caption: a strong hook, a clear call-to-action, relevant hashtags and keywords.

By following these points, you can effectively grab your audience's attention, build trust, and drive more engagement and conversions.

Caption Structure for Maximum Engagement:

[Strong Hook Statement/Question]

[Expanded Value Statement]

[3-4 Bullet Points of Key Takeaways]

[Call-to-Action]
#luxury #luxurylifestyle [3-5 targeted hashtags]

Use this as a guide when writing your captions. Get creative, put your own spin on it, continue testing and use what works Utilize AI like ChatGPT to give you ideas and aid in the creation process.

Hashtags

While some argue that hashtags are no longer as crucial, many social media experts still recommend utilizing them as part of your strategy. Even if you can achieve great reach without them, using relevant hashtags can still be beneficial.

When choosing hashtags, it's best to focus on those that are less saturated, typically between 50,000 to 100,000 uses. Highly competitive, million-use hashtags are less likely to help your content get discovered.

You can also use tools like Hashtag Guru and Boost App Social to optimize your hashtags. Your best chance at finding great hashtags though, are to look at competitors in your niche. Analyze their best performing posts

In addition to hashtags, keywords are also an important consideration for the Instagram algorithm. Be sure to incorporate relevant keywords not only in your on-screen text, but also in your caption. Repeating the same keywords 4-5 times throughout your caption can help signal to the algorithm what your content is about.

If your caption is on the shorter side, you can include additional keywords below your hashtags. This ensures you're optimizing your content for better discoverability among your target audience.

Strategically using a combination of thoughtfully selected hashtags and keywords, can improve the chances of your Instagram content being placed in front of the right people, helping you build a stronger presence and drive more engagement.

Trending Audio

Trending audio refers to any audio that the platform has highlighted as being popular. Using a trending audio is crucial if you want to reach a wider audience, as Instagram is more likely to push your video out to more users when you leverage trending audio.

You can identify a trending audio by the diagonal up-arrow icon. Clicking on this arrow will take you to all the videos using that specific audio, allowing you to see how many times it has been used.

For the best results, it's recommended to use trending audios that have less than 5,000 or up to 10,000 uses. The ideal scenario is when the "original" video using the audio has over 1 million views and has received recent comments within the last few days, as this indicates the audio is likely to continue gaining momentum.

While scrolling through Instagram, be sure to save any videos, audios, or trends that you find interesting or potentially useful. You can save Reels into folders and save your favorite audios to use in your own content later.

By strategically using trending audio, you can leverage the platform's algorithm to increase the visibility and reach of your Instagram Reels, helping you connect with a wider audience.

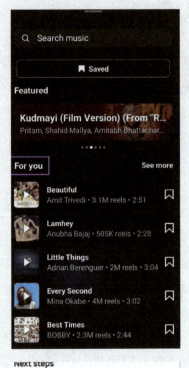

One way to find trending audio is by tapping on audio, scroll to for you and search for trending audio.

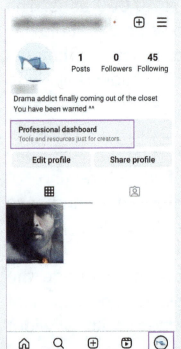
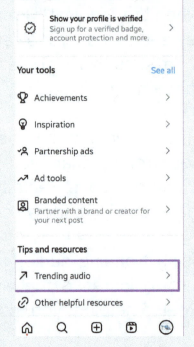

Or you can go to the **professional dashboard** and select trending audio

The best way to find appropriate audios is to look at the competitors that are using trending audios.

Stories for Luxury Pages

Instagram Stories are a crucial component of your marketing strategy that shouldn't be overlooked. Your audience is interested in you and what you have to offer, so it's important to engage with them through your Stories. They serve a different purpose than Reels in the luxury niche. Use them to:
1. Create FOMO (Fear of Missing Out)
2. Share time-sensitive information
3. Drive engagement through polls and questions
4. Showcase exclusive products/services
5. Preview upcoming content

Most people use stories just to repost their main posts. By doing these instead you fully utilize the stories on your page

You want to mix up your story content like this::
- 70% Educational/Value
- 20% Engagement drivers
- 10% Promotional

Example of a story post with a freebie offer

In regards to Call to actions, we are going to target our audience using different types

1. Soft CTAs (Early Stage):
    - "Discover more luxury insights"
    - "Explore our curated collections"
    - "Join the conversation"

2. Value-Based CTAs (Mid Stage):
    - "Access exclusive luxury insights"
    - "Learn proven investment strategies"
    - "Unlock premium content"

3. Direct CTAs (Warm Audience):
    - "Secure your spot"
    - "Join our private network"
    - "Schedule your consultation"

Instagram Highlihts

You can use these stories to promote your products, including providing a direct link to make purchases easy for your customers.

Once you start creating helpful and engaging Story content, it's a good idea to create Highlights for your profile. Recommended Highlight categories include:

- Your results
- Your story/your 'why'
- Frequently asked questions
- Information about your freeble or digital products
- Testimonials

Building a connection with your audience through these types of Story posts can be highly beneficial, as a significant portion of your sales may come directly from your Stories.

By consistently posting to your Stories and leveraging Highlights, you can effectively connect with your audience, showcase your offerings, and drive sales for your business.

Posting Strategy and Timing

Best times to post based on the day:
- Monday: 3 am, 11 am, 12 pm
- Tuesday: 8 am, 9 am, 10 am
- Wednesday: 9 am, 11 am, 1 pm
- Thursday: 6 am, 11 am, 12 pm
- Friday: 11 am, 2 pm, 4 pm
- Saturday: 9 am, 10 am, 5 pm
- Sunday: 5 am, 1 pm, 2 pm

- Reels: 1-2 posts per day
- Stories: 3-5 per day

- Carousels however, don't offer as much engagement if your page is still young but 2 posts per week is sufficient.

Organization is key and we offer Content Creator Essentials that can help keep everything organized and flow flawlessly.

Viral Video

Before hitting that upload button on your latest post, it's good to take a step back and critically evaluate its potential performance. By considering a few key questions, you can ensure your content is primed for maximum engagement and impact.

1. Will people actually stop and look at this for a few seconds?
   - Ask yourself if the visuals, opening hook, and overall video flow are captivating enough to grab your audience's attention.
2. Will people want to share this to their story or send to a friend?
   - Assess whether your content is entertaining, inspiring, or informative enough for your audience to want to share it with their own followers.
3. Will people want to comment and give their opinion?
   - Determine if your video encourages discussion, invites questions, or sparks a desire for your audience to engage by leaving comments.
4. Will people want to save this for later and come back to?
   - Evaluate if your content provides lasting value that your audience would want to revisit or reference in the future.
5. Does this provide value and substance?
   - Ensure that your video delivers genuine value to your target audience, whether it's educational, motivational, or simply delightful.

If you can confidently answer "yes" to all of these questions, then you've got a winning piece of content on your hands.

Chapter 4
The Algorithm and Avoiding Common Mistakes

Use the algorithm to your advantage and get
more out of your luxury theme pages

Algorithms

"One of the main misconceptions we want to clear up is the existence of "The Algorithm." Instagram doesn't have one algorithm that oversees what people do and don't see on the app. We use a variety of algorithms, classifiers, and processes, each with its own purpose."

-Adam Mosseri (head of Instagram)

FEED/STORY

EXPLORE

PENALTY

REELS

Feed/Story

Let's break down how the algorithm works and how to optimize your luxury content accordingly.
Instagram's algorithm assigns different weights to various interactions:

Highest Value Actions:
1. Saves
2. Shares
3. Comments
4. Watch time
5. Likes

Notice how likes are at the bottom? Even so likes are a great way to gauge just how much engagement you're getting.

To maximize your use of the algorithm:
- Create content that deserves to be saved and shared
- Encourage meaningful discussion
- Build natural engagement patterns

Feed and Story

are ranked based on

Primary Signals

1. Initial engagement velocity
2. Account authority score
3. User relationship strength
4. Content relevance score
5. Time decay factor

Secondary Signals

1. Caption length and quality
2. Hashtag relevance
3. Image/video quality
4. Account activity pattern
5. Engagement consistency

Primary Signals:
The Instagram algorithm places significant emphasis on several primary signals when determining content distribution and visibility.

The initial engagement velocity of a post is a crucial factor, as the speed and volume of likes and comments received in the first hour are key triggers for broader distribution. The platform closely monitors the acceleration patterns of early engagement, with the first 30-60 minutes being particularly critical. Posts that garner a rapid initial response are more likely to be surfaced to a wider audience.

Another important signal is the account authority score, which is built through a history of consistent, quality content. This score reflects the overall engagement patterns of the account, taking into account factors like follower quality, activity levels, account age, and past post performance.

The strength of the user's relationships with their followers also plays a role. The algorithm considers the frequency and nature of previous interactions, such as comment exchanges and direct message history. Mutual engagement patterns and the strength of the account's community connections contribute to this user relationship signal.

By strategically optimizing for these primary signals - initial engagement velocity, account authority, and user relationship strength - content creators can improve their chances of achieving greater visibility and distribution on the Instagram platform.

Secondary Signals
Caption Length and Quality:
The algorithm assesses the optimal length and overall quality of the caption. This includes the use of relevant keywords, readability and formatting, the effectiveness of any call-to-action, and the natural language patterns employed.

Hashtag Relevance:
The accuracy and relevance of the hashtags used are evaluated. This encompasses the volume of appropriate tags, the balance between niche-specific and broader hashtags, the historical performance of those tags, and how they align with any trending topics.

Image/Video Quality:
The technical specifications of the visual content, such as resolution, clarity, and composition, are analyzed. The algorithm also considers the overall aesthetic appeal, mobile optimization, and adherence to platform guidelines.

Account Activity Pattern:
The algorithm examines the consistency of the account's posting frequency, its engagement with other profiles, response rate to comments, daily activity distribution, and overall platform presence.

Engagement Consistency:
Finally, the algorithm assesses the stability and quality of the account's engagement rates over time, the nature of the engaging accounts, the pattern of interaction types, and the overall sustainability and natural growth of engagement.

MORE ON THE STORY ALGORITHM

Completion Rate is a crucial metric, as it measures how many viewers watch your story all the way to the end. Higher completion rates signal to the algorithm that your content is engaging and of high quality, which in turn boosts the distribution of your future stories.

Forward and Backward Taps also play a key role. Quick forward taps, indicating disinterest, can hurt your visibility, while backward taps, showing engagement, can actually boost your story's distribution. The rate and patterns of these taps significantly impact how the algorithm will surface your content.

Next Story Behavior is another important factor. If viewers continue to your next story, it signals strong retention and will positively influence your overall visibility. Conversely, high exit rates between your stories can negatively impact future story distribution.

Explore Algorithm

To consistently land on people's Explore pages, you need to focus on several key factors:

1. Engagement and Interaction:
   - Increase organic engagement on your posts through high-quality content and interactions.
   - Engage with your existing audience by encouraging comments, **starting conversations**, and using effective calls-to-action (CTAs).
   - Building a highly engaged following is crucial to improving your chances of appearing on the Explore page.

2. Relevance and Personalization:
   - The Explore algorithm considers whether the user has interacted with your content in the past.
   - Ensure that your content is relevant to the specific interests and preferences of your target audience.
   - Use niche-specific keywords, hashtags, and branding to signal the relevance of your content.

3. Consistency and Collaboration:
   - Maintain a consistent theme and topic across all your content.
   - Engage and collaborate with other accounts within your niche to cross-promote and expand your reach.

Focusing on these key elements you can increase your chances of appearing on the Instagram Explore page, which can significantly boost your visibility and attract new followers.

Reels Algorithm

The Reels feed is primarily built to show you entertaining content, with a special emphasis on discovering new and emerging creators. The algorithm determines what to show you based on four main factors:

1. Your Personal Viewing Habits
What matters most is how you interact with Reels, especially which ones you watch completely and engage with recently.

2. Creator History
While Reels often shows content from creators you don't follow, the algorithm may prioritize creators whose content you've interacted with before, similar to how the Explore page works.

3. Reel Characteristics
The algorithm analyzes elements like the music used, the content itself (using AI), and how popular the Reel is overall.

4. Creator Performance
The algorithm considers how well the creator's account has been performing lately, including their overall engagement rates and how other users have interacted with their content in recent weeks.

This system is specifically designed to help you discover entertaining content, often from creators you haven't encountered before. Understanding this system gives you an advantage in your content creation.

Summary for utilizing the algorithm:

- Structure videos to maintain viewer interest throughout, using hooks and maintaining narrative flow
- Develop themed content sequences that keep viewers coming back for more information
- Maintain a regular posting schedule to keep audience engaged and satisfy algorithm requirements
- Create content that naturally encourages back-and-forth interaction through questions and discussion points
- Foster connections between followers by facilitating discussions and creating community posts
- Use high-quality visuals that reflects the luxury lifestyle
- Make sure your videos are short and good so they watch it more than once
- Research and implement relevant luxury and wealth-focused hashtags
- Write captions that are both engaging and optimized for algorithm visibility
- Maintain optimal posting times based on audience activity patterns
- Regularly analyze content performance to refine strategy
-Interactive features like polls and quizzes can significantly boost engagement metrics and indicate active audience involvement, which the algorithm recognizes and rewards with increased visibility.

Audience Hacking

Here are tipson how to optimize your audience:

1: Make sure to post on the USA timezone.
2:Make sure that all of your content is made on English language
3: Put USA or New York Location on every post. This will tell Instagram what audience to push the content out to.

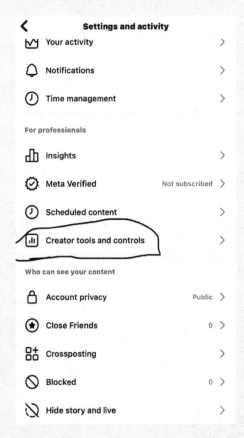

This is a **SECRET** way to do this method and it has a 100% success rate:
Go to your Instagram settings
Go to Creator tools & controls. If you put your professional account on Business, it should say Business tools & controls, but it's the same thing
Go to Minimum age
In the By country, click Add and choose the audiences you don't want to be able to see your account.
Set the minimum age to 25

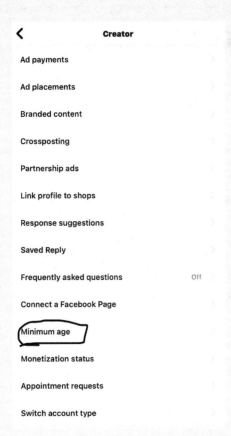

Use this method to transform the audience you currently to the audience you desire.

How to make sharable content?

In the realm of luxury content, creating shareable posts isn't just an option, it's essential for exponential growth. When your content resonates so deeply that followers feel compelled to share it, you unlock a powerful chain reaction of organic exposure that can transform your Instagram presence.

Each share exposes your content to an entirely new audience. What begins as a single post can evolve into thousands of new impressions through story shares, reposts, and saves.

To create content that your audience wants to share, your posts must embody specific qualities that resonate with the luxury mindset:
They must embody aesthetic excellence by using impeccable visuals that reflect a luxurious lifestyle. Good use of colours and aesthetic ambience is vital. The content can be

1. Useful
2. Entertaining
3. Inspirational
4.Thought-Provoking
5.Controversial
6. Relatable

The most powerful element is relatability. Relatibility is the gold standard for making shareable content

Avoiding Common Mistakes:

- Only use fonts that are easy to read on top of your video. If people have to squint or strain, or if the words blend in with the background, they'll scroll right by.
- Maintain consistent fonts, colors, and visuals across your content to build a cohesive luxury aesthetic.
- Keep your reels between 5-11 seconds for optimal engagement.
- Avoid overdoing it with filters or using overly abstract effects. Stick to a clean, refined look.
- Position text in easy-to-read areas, away from profile info or buttons.
- Regularly "Save As Draft" and back up your footage to avoid losing progress.
- Stay disciplined with a regular posting cadence to keep your audience engaged.
- Respond to comments on other pages but when it comes to your page respond to only one or two
- Steer Clear of Fake Followers and Engagement. Never purchase fake followers or engage in bot-driven activities like buying likes. Fake followers do not interact with your content, causing the algorithm to view it as low-quality

- Avoid using third-party apps that require you to log into your Instagram or TikTok account. These apps can potentially result in account bans, restrictions, or hacks

- The "boost post" feature on Instagram is often an ineffective way to promote your content. It lacks the advanced targeting and optimization capabilities. Boosting posts is typically a waste of money if not set up correctly

Chapter 5 Monetization Mastery

How can we earn from these luxury theme pages? Sales is an essential skill that takes immense practice to master.

Selling digital products

Here is a list of great Marketplaces and Platforms to sell digital products on:

1. Mighty Networks
2. ConvertKit
3. Kajabi
4. Udemy
5. Shopify
6. Classful
7. Amazon
8. Etsy
9. Sellfy
10. Gumroad
11. Podia
12. Sendowl
13. Payhip
14. Squarespace
15. Easy Digital Downloads
16. BigCommerce
17. StanStore

There are so many marketplaces and platforms to sell your digital products. It is a similar setup in all of them but for this example I will use Gumroad.

Step 1 — Sign Up on the Gumroad website
This is easy to do. All you need is an email. And that's it. Click
on Start selling button and sign up using your email.

After signing up this is what your dashboard looks like. Your
name will appear on the top left side of the dashboard. It will
also give you some help getting started.

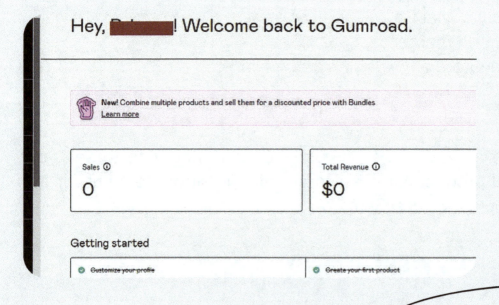

Step2

Local/Currency Settings- If you see on the left menu then down at the bottom there is Settings option.

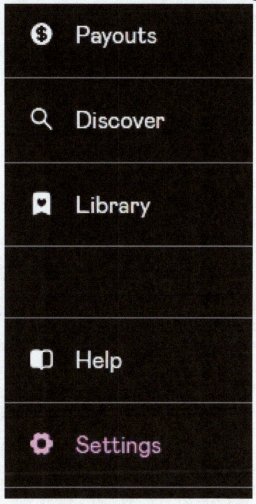

Now to set your local timing as it is useful while doing email marketing and receiving notifications. Also set up your currency.

Note that when you select the language then it only changes the language of your creator dashboard. And not your product descriptions, names, or any updates.

Settings

(Settings)   Profile   Team   Payments   Password   Third-party analytics   Advanced

Local

Language

English

Time zone

-08:00 | Pacific Time (US & Canada)

Sell in...

$ (US Dollars)

The time zone you select will also affect your sales and following dashboards. There you can see a "Sell in.." option. It lets you choose the default currency for your products. Gumroad charges customers in USD at the current exchange rate during the purchase. For currency — You can change that to anything of your choice.

Currency available — GBP, Euro, Yen, Rupees, Australian Dollars, Canadian Dollars, Swiss Franc, Korean Won, Polish zloty etc.

Also make sure you have added your -
1. Username
2. Name
3. Bio
4. Logo

If you want you can connect your account to social media accounts as well.

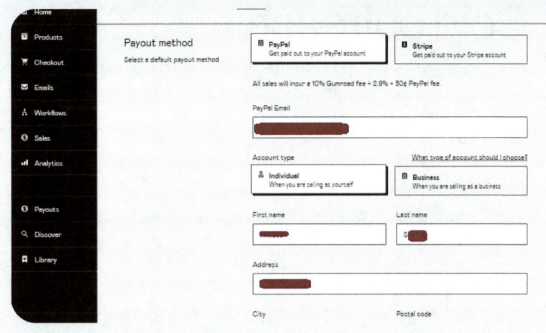

Step 3 — Payment Method

This is the exciting part. Once the setup is complete, you'll be paid every week!

Before uploading anything to your store make sure that you have your payment methods in place.

.Some people will have a Bank transfer option as well.

- For PayPal: All sales will incur a 10% Gumroad fee + 2.9% + 30¢ PayPal fee.
- For Stripe: All sales will incur a 10% Gumroad fee.

So many free solutions are there and it takes only a few minutes to set up.

You have the product.

You have the audience

Now get marketing!

Cold outreach

A great way to get clients is using cold outreach using Instagram DMs to get new creators to buy your products. Here's how:

- Compile a list of potential instagram profiles
- Craft a personalized direct message that highlights the unique value of your products.
- Emphasize how your video clips or presets can solve their specific content creation challenges.
- Offer a free sample or trial of your products to showcase their quality and features.
- Encourage customers to provide feedback.
- Be ready to negotiate and be prepared to address any concerns or questions your potential customers may have
- Highlight the exclusivity, quality, and time-saving benefits of your offerings.
- Leverage social proof, such as testimonials and case studies, to build trust and credibility.
- Consider offering flexible and transparent pricing options, such as individual product sales, bundles, or mentorship subscription models.
- Ensure your website or sales platform provides a seamless, user-friendly purchasing process.
- Offer secure payment options and provide excellent customer service throughout the transaction.
- Follow up with customers after the sale to gather feedback and nurture the relationship, usually done with an email.
- Incentivize your satisfied customers to refer your products to their peers and connections.
- Offer exclusive discounts, free products, or other rewards for successful referrals.

Freebie Selling

A **Free Digital Product**(or **lead magnet**) is an incentive you offer your target audience in exchange for their email address. There are plenty of free products types you can offer. A mini guide, eBook, mini course, just to name a few.

01

List Building:
A free offer is an excellent way to grow your email list, which is a critical asset for any online business. Each person who signs up for your email list becomes a potential lead that you can nurture over time.

02

Trust and Authority:
By offering valuable content or a helpful freebie, you establish trust with your audience and position your brand as an authority in your industry. This goodwill makes people more receptive to your future recommendations and offerings.

03

Securing Your Audience:
In the event your social media accounts are ever suspended or banned, having an email list ensures you can still maintain direct communication with your audience, preventing the loss of your hard-earned customer base.

04

Business Automation:
Email marketing is the key to running your digital product business on autopilot. By building an email list, you can create a reliable and scalable system for making sales even when you're not actively working.

05

Lead Nurturing:
Once you've collected leads through your free offer, you can use email marketing to nurture those leads over time. By providing additional valuable content, sharing success stories, and guiding them through the buyer's journey, you can increase the likelihood of sales conversions.

06

Long-Term Relationships:
Lead magnets are not just about immediate conversions; they are a tool for building lasting relationships with your customers. Through ongoing communication and valuable content, you can keep your audience engaged and turn one-time buyers into repeat customers.

Your freebie should provide a sneak peek into the value and solutions your paid offering will deliver, but without revealing the entire package. It should wet your audience's appetite, leaving them eager to learn more.

When crafting your free guide, focus on addressing a specific problem or challenge that your ideal customer is facing. Offer them a solution that holds genuine value and solves a pressing issue. This will incentivize your target audience to opt-in and download your freebie, growing your email list in the process.

There are various types of free products you can consider, such as:

- Webinars or mini-courses
- Concise guides or e-books
- Templates, checklists, or listicles
- Short, informative training videos

To find inspiration, take a look at what your competitors are offering as freebies. Use these as a starting point, but be sure to put your own unique spin on the content to differentiate your offering.

For a quick and easy solution, you can consider using pre-made lead magnet templates available on platforms like Etsy or Canva. Simply customize the template with your own branding and content, and you'll have a professional-looking freebie ready to go.

If you'd prefer making your own freebie here are some tips:

- The freebie should deliver meaningful value, not just be a gimmick giveaway. Offer something like actionable advice.

- Focus on helping with an urgent pain point your audience has.

- Give a preview of your paid products

- Include activities to engage readers to implement advice.

- Cover a narrow slice of a larger topic to hook interest for the full product.

- Direct them to purchase the complete product to gain more.

- Subtly showcase your brand, website, and offers in the freebie design. Lead capture: Collect reader emails in exchange for the free download.

Xeuraura.VIP Exclusive Filters

$0

 IT'S FREE

Get for free

Example of a freebie product

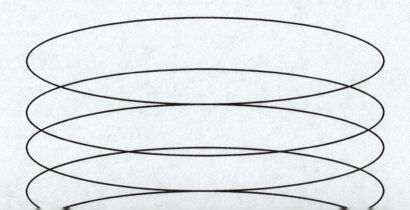

The best performing digital products in the luxury theme bpage niche are:

Editing Presets and LUTs:

- Preset filters, LUTs (Look-Up Tables), and editing tools tailored for luxury-themed imagery.
- Allow users to achieve a consistent, high-end visual style across their Instagram content.

Social Media Content Kits:

- This would include luxury clips, graphics, captions and templates used for luxury clips
- This saves time and effort for users who want to consistently post high-quality content.

Guides:

- This can include n-depth guides on building a luxury theme page, crafting and editing compelling content, and growing a luxury-focused audience.
- Topics could include social media strategy, marketing, and creating an overall high-end aesthetic.

You are not limited to these. Try to think outside the box and make something unique!

Chapter 6
Email Marketing

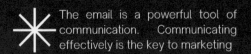

The email is a powerful tool of communication. Communicating effectively is the key to marketing

Email list

Building an Effective Email List and Marketing Strategy

The foundation of a successful digital product business lies in building and nurturing an email list. Here are the key steps to leverage email marketing effectively:

Step 1: Build Your List
Collect email addresses from interested individuals through sign-up forms, giveaways, and social media interactions. Offer a valuable freebie or lead magnet in exchange for their contact information.

Step 2: Segment Your Audience
Divide your email list into targeted groups based on criteria such as interests, buying stage, and engagement levels. This allows you to send more personalized and relevant communications.

Step 3: Create Compelling Content
Craft email content that is informative, entertaining, and valuable to your audience. Share personal stories, provide useful tips and insights, and highlight the benefits of your digital products in addressing their pain points.

Step 4: Focus on Pain Points
Empathize with the struggles and challenges faced by your subscribers, and position your digital products as the solution to their problems. Build trust and credibility by demonstrating your understanding of their needs.

Step 5: Use Effective Calls-to-Action

Include clear and compelling calls-to-action in your emails, prompting subscribers to take desired actions, such as making a purchase, visiting your website, or engaging with your content.

Additional Strategies for Email Marketing Success:

- Personalize emails by incorporating subscriber data and past behavior
- Test and optimize different email formats, subject lines, and send times
- Monitor key metrics like open rates, click-through rates, and conversion rates
- Ensure compliance with email marketing regulations and laws
- Consistently provide value to your subscribers to strengthen relationships

By implementing these email marketing best practices, you can effectively nurture your audience, drive sales, and build a thriving digital product business.

Email flows

These are automated sequences of emails that are sent to your subscribers on a predetermined schedule. These email flows are a powerful tool for digital product businesses, as they allow you to nurture leads and drive sales on autopilot.

Confirmation Emails
The first step in setting up email flows is to create confirmation emails for your digital products. These emails are sent immediately after a subscriber signs up for your freebie or purchases a paid product. The confirmation email should include:
1. Download links for the digital product(s)
2. A personalized message from you
By having these confirmation emails set up, you can ensure a seamless delivery of your digital products and establish a positive first impression with your new subscribers or customers.

How It Works
1. Someone signs up for your freebie:
  - They receive a confirmation email with the freebie download link and a brief message from you.
2. Someone purchases your paid digital product:
  - They receive a confirmation email with the product download link and a personalized message from you.

This automated process ensures a smooth experience for your customers and lays the foundation for your email marketing workflows.
By setting up these confirmation emails and other automated email flows, you can free up your time and focus on creating high-quality digital products and content. The email sequences will continue to nurture your leads and drive sales on autopilot, allowing your business to run more efficiently and profitably.

The following are example email templates
Freebie Email

Example 1:
👎 Subject: Exclusive Offer - Free Download of [Product/Service]

Dear [Name],
I hope this email finds you well. I am writing to offer you an exclusive opportunity to download [Product/Service] for free.
[Product/Service] is a [Description of Product/Service] that can help with
[Benefits of Product/Service]. We believe that this product/service has the potential to be
valuable for your business and would like to offer you the opportunity to try it out for free.
This offer is only available to a select few and we believe that you would benefit
greatly from this product/service. To access your free download, simply click on the link
below and follow the instructions:

[Link to Download]
We hope that you find this product/service valuable and would love to hear your feedback. Please don't hesitate to reach out if you have any questions or if there is anything that we can help with.

Sincerely,
[Your Name]

Example 2:

🔨 Subject: [Product/Service] - Free Download Offer

Dear [Name],

I hope this email finds you well. I am writing to offer you a free download of
[Product/Service].
[Product/Service] is a [Description of Product/Service] that can help with
[Benefits of Product/Service]. We believe that this product/service has the potential to be
valuable for your business and would like to offer you the opportunity to try it out for free.
To access your free download, simply click on the link below and follow the
instructions:

[Link to Download]
We are confident that you will find this product/service valuable and would be
happy to
answer any questions or provide further information. Please don't hesitate to
reach out
if you have any questions or if there is anything that we can help with.

Best regards,
[Your Name]

ANNOUNCEMENT EMAILS

♣ Subject: Free Download: [problem download solves or download name]

Hi there [NAME],

If you need a bit of help [insert what your free download helps with], I recommend you go here
right now [LINK] and get this [free report / free software, etc.].
It [helps you / shows you how to]:

□ Benefit #1
□ Benefit #2
□ Benefit #3
Click here to grab it [LINK].
Just do it quickly because it won't be available long.

To Your Success,
[Your NAME]

FOLLOW-UP
🔨 Subject: Free Download Reminder: [problem you're solving]

Dear [NAME],

Did you see this yet?
This is just a quick reminder that you can download [insert what they can
download]...absolutely
free for a limited time.
It [helps you / shows you how to]:
Benefit1
Benefit2
Benefit3
Go get it while you still can!

To Your Success,
[YOUR NAME]

LAST CALL
📌 Subject: Last call for this free [insert what it is]

Dear [NAME],

[There are just a few hours left OR whatever time is left]
to get your [free copy of
XXXX]. I didn't want you to miss out on this, so grab it
here now [LINK].
Get it now before it's too late. And hey, let me know what
you think. I lways
appreciate the feedback.

To your success,
[YOUR NAME]

Paid Offer Email

Subject: Here is your [Product Name]!

Hi [Customer Name],

Thank you for purchasing [Product Name]! I'm so excited for you to dive in. I can't wait to see what you do and how your life changes with this! Here is your download

[DOWNLOAD LINK]

Shoot me a DM on IG [include hyperlink] when you get a chance to let me know that you've taken this step! I'd love to connect & celebrate with you!

[Your Name]

Setting up your email flow

Once you've established your confirmation emails, you can begin to set up your email flow. Initially, you will want to create just **one email flow** for those who opt in for your freebie. While there isn't a single correct way to structure your flow, it's beneficial to include the following elements in your first few emails:

- Value: Provide useful information or insights.
- Introduction: Share who you are and what you stand for.
-Your Story: Connect with your audience by telling your personal journey.
-Product Promotion: Introduce your products or services subtly.

Here's an example timeline for your email flow:

1. Welcome & Freebie: Send this email immediately after they opt in.
2. Nurturing Email Send this 24-48 hours after the first email.
3. Value Email: Follow up with this email 24-48 hours after the second email.
4. The Big Offer Email: Send this email 24-48 hours after the third email.

If you need assistance with setting up your optimal email flow for your freebie, consider checking out additional resources like ChatGPT for guidance. Remember to test and don't be afraid to make mistakes at first.

Tip for Inspiration

It's a good idea to subscribe to other creators' email lists to gather inspo for your email flow, but remember not to copy their content directly.

By following these guidelines, you can create an effective email flow that engages your audience and promotes your brand effectively.

Setting up your email flow

Subject: Are you ready for your first $3-5k months?

Have you had a chance to check out my free guide? If so, and you are ready to use a DFY digital product to get your own passive income business off the ground, I want to invite you to purchase my [Product Name].
[INSERT FEEDBACK ON YOUR DIGITAL PRODUCT HERE - CAN ADD THESE LATER] With [Product Name] you will learn everything you need to know about getting a profitable DFY digital product business up and running in the next 30 days (and enjoying $3k, $5k, and even $10k+ months!) You will get: My digital product to use, modify, and resell as your own A step-by-step process for getting your online shop set up with ease and automation My content strategies for marketing your product in just a few hours a week PLUS my plug-and-play email templates so your automated system can bring in daily sales even in your sleep! This is an entire business ready for you to fully make your own and fully profit from. Why? Because I know just how life-changing a stream of passive income like this can be, and you can do it too! [Your Name]

Setting up your email flow

EMAIL # 2

Subject: You are closer to making money than you realize

Hi [Customer Name],

I want you to know that you are closer to having a profitable passive income business, and your first $3-10k months, than you realize. Whether you are already a business-owner, or have zero experience... Whether you work a 9-to-5, or are a student... Whether you have a large social media presence, or are starting from scratch... You CAN leverage just a few hours a week to bring in income that provides for your family and changes your life. With just one digital product and an automated system for driving traffic to it, you can build a highly profitable business from home in just a few hours a week. And with a DONE-FOR-YOU, or DFY, digital product, you don't even need to have any special expertise or create your own product from scratch either. This is why I created [Product Name - include hyperlink] - to help you get your biz up and running FAST using the steps inside and my plug-and-play template. Download it, then tweak it and make it your own so you can resell it for FULL profit. Start bringing in $97 sales every day, multiple times a day, even in your sleep and just as importantly, enjoy the freedom that comes with itReady to get started? Your next step is to purchase [Product Name] here [include hyperlink]. And don't forget you can always shoot me a DM [include hyperlink] if you have questions!

[Your Name]

Setting up your email flow

EMAIL # 3

Subject: Another [insert $ amount] made while [insert activity]

 Hi [Customer Name],

And just like that, another [insert income made here] today while _____! This is the beauty of digital products - having a business that runs and makes money for you while you're out having an actual life! Are you ready to start leveraging just a few hours a week to bring in continual passive income in the same way? If so, your next step is purchasing [Product Name], where I've already done the legwork and created the product for you. You can click here [insert hyperlink] to learn more about [Product Name] and get started now. I am rooting for you and can't wait to see how your life changes with this!

[Your Name]

Setting up your email flow

EMAIL # 4

Subject: [Insert $ amount] in _____ days In the last ___ days,

I've made [insert $ amount] using nothing more than one digital product. I want you to imagine this being YOU. Imagine getting notifications throughout the week while you're with your kids... or binging Netflix... or folding laundry... or even sleeping! Notifications letting you know that you just made another sale on a digital product (that you didn't even have to create from scratch!) all because someone else stumbled across a Reel and decided they wanted in on this kind of life too. One product bringing in thousands a week while you're just working 2-3 hours all so that you can spend the rest of your time enjoying the people and things you love. If you haven't already, I want to challenge you to take a bold step. Purchase [Product Name] for [price] today. Change your life. Build a business that can run on autopilot and give you the time and freedom you've been dreaming of.

[Your Name] Don't forget, you can always shoot me a DM [insert hyperlink] on Instagram

Setting up your email flow

SECOND EMAIL FLOW

Later on down the road, you may want to have a second email flow, specifically for people who purchase your paid offers. This is primarily if you are also offering other products that you want to sell as **add-ons** or **upsells**.

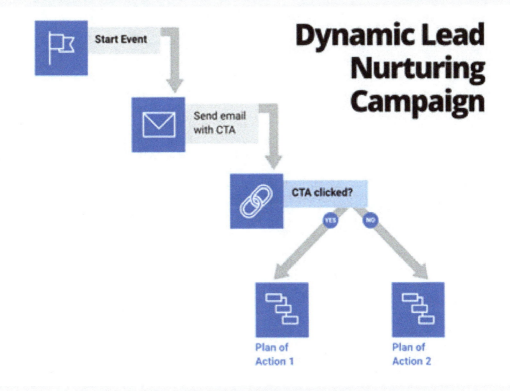

IMPORTANT: Make sure to test your freebie and paid offer before you start creating content to attract your dream customers. Do this by opting in for your freebie and purchasing your paid offer.

There are platforms you can utilize to automate the email marketing process. Gumroad has a built in email marketing system. You can use
1. ActiveCampaign
2. GetResponse
3. Brevo
4. Zoho Campaigns
5. MailerLite
6. Benchmark
7. Mailchimp
To name a few...

Develop Your Marketing Strategy

Write down your step by step structure on how you plan to use email marketing, from getting eyes on your product to making the sale.

Chapter 7 Community Building

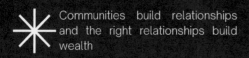

Communities build relationships and the right relationships build wealth

While some may argue that building a community without a visible face is challenging, it can actually be easier than you think, provided you apply the right strategies.

There are so many platforms you can use to build a community

The following are apps and platforms you can use to build communities

Instagram
Facebook Groups
Discord- Whop
Telegram
Skool
Swarm
Slack

Consistency Is Key

Staying consistent is the foundation of building a community for your page. In the early stages, it's recommended to post at least once a day, if not more. Aim for 2-3 Reels and 6-8 Stories per day to signal to the algorithm that you're an active, serious user. This regular presence will help establish trust and reliability with your audience over time.

As your following grows, you can gradually reduce the posting frequency, potentially down to 1 Reel every 2 days, while maintaining a consistent schedule.

Branding and Value Delivery

Branding is crucial, even for a faceless brand. Ensure that your visual identity, including your Instagram feed, Digital Store, and email communications, is cohesive and visually appealing. Avoid clashing colors, fonts, and elements that can make your brand appear unprofessional and forgettable.

Importantly, remember that Instagram is primarily a value-driven platform. Your content should focus on providing genuine value to your audience, addressing their pain points and educating them on solutions. This approach will help you stand out and give your audience a compelling reason to follow and engage with your brand.

The Power of Storytelling

Your personal story is arguably the most important aspect of your branding, as it's something that no one else can replicate. Storytelling has the power to connect your audience with your brand on an emotional level, building trust and loyalty much faster.

Share your journey, the challenges you've overcome, and the triumphs that led you to this point. Your audience will resonate with your authenticity and be drawn to your brand as a result.

Cultivate, then Convert

In the early stages of building your community, your primary focus should be on selflessly serving your audience. Shift your mindset to understand that your audience only cares about what you can do for them, not your own personal experiences or preferences.

Provide value by answering their burning questions, educating them on solutions to their problems, and sharing your best tips and tricks. This "serve first, sell later" approach will help you establish trust and credibility, laying the foundation for future sales.

By consistently applying these strategies, you can confidently build a thriving community for your faceless brand, laying the groundwork for a successful and sustainable digital product business.

BONUSES

THE HOOK

Your hook is KEY. This is a quick, catchy phrase or word to get your
ideal audience to stop scrolling and pay attention.

You should have a strong hook in two places on your reel:

1. On-screen text: The first words your viewer will see when scrolling by your reel. You have no more than 3 seconds to grab your viewers attention.
The job of this hook is to get them to stop their scroll and watch your reel.

2. The start of your caption: The first word(s) of your caption should be a showstopper. The job of this hook is to get them to actually read your caption. The better the caption is -> the more time spent reading it -> the more watch time your reel will get -> the more your reel will be pushed to more people.
I have some hook examples for you on the next page.

Example Hooks

"Here's a shortcut for___" (how to go from A to B)

"How to___in (x) minutes" (insert your audiences pain points)

"The fastest way to___" (achieve a specific goal)

"TOP5___" (insert a specific goal)

"Major mistakes most___make" (person of your niche)

"Step by step guide to___" (insert a feasible goal)

"Why doing ___ (insert most common thing) will not help ___ (desire)!"

"Do this to___" (how to go from A to B)

"5 toxic mistakes to avoid if you want___" (desire)

"The biggest misconception about___" (bust a myth)

"You've been doing ___wrong your entire life!" (a specific topic)

"3 rules to unlock___" (a specific outcome)

"5 ways to___" (achieve a desired outcome)

"This hack will blow your mind!"

"My journey from 0 to___" (name your current status)

"The real secret about___" (a specific topic)

"You won't believe this hack!"

___

"My secret strategy to"___

"Fastest way to"___

"If you want to___ you need to try this!"

"Top 5 tips for"___

"How to master"___

More HOOKS

5 surprising facts about"__

"If you want to achieve X, you need to__"

"The most effective strategies for"__

"My top resources for"__

"The biggest misconceptions about"__

"The most overlooked ways to"__

"The #1 thing you need to know about"__

"I never thought I could"__

"The best advice I ever received about"__

"Behind the scenes of"__

"The one thing you're doing wrong that's holding you back from (goal])"

"Are you tired of (problem)? Here's how to fix it."

"Don't make these mistakes when (task or goal)"

"The truth about (common misconception or belief)"

"The (adjective) way to improve your (skill or task)"

"(Number) things you didn't know you could do with (product or service)"

"The ultimate guide to mastering (skill or task)"

"The best (skill or activity) hacks for (task or problem)"

(Number) reasons why (topic) is important"

""The Dos and Don'ts of"__"

If you want to achieve X, you need to__"

"The most common mistakes when"__

Even more HOOKS
"The surprising truth about
"The secret to"__
"Top 5 tools for"__
"The ultimate checklist for"__"
"How to overcome"__
"The top trends in"__
"The most effective strategies for__"
"How I got from X to Y Ways to get your first"__
"Stop doing this if you want X Steal my __"
"Stop making these mistakes"__
"5 facts you didn't know about"__
"3 reasons why you need to start"__
"The science behind"__
"My top resources for"__
"How to supercharge your"__
"The top 5 things you need to know about
"The secret to achieving __"
"Behind the scenes of"__"
"The most common mistakes when"__
"How I got from X to Y"__
"The ultimate guide to"__
"A step-by-step guide to__

THE SYSTEM

Once you have created a successful luxury theme page. The next step is to create more luxury pages and monetize them. At some point you should look to hiring people to run these pages for you. You can use platforms like Fiverr or Upwork to hire them.

This is how to build a theme page system that will be bringing in passive income every month. The concept of faceless theme pages is a gold mine and while it is here we need to use it. Later on, you can branch into other niches that you think may profitable. Using the knowledge you have now, you are fully equipped to manage and monetize your very own luxury theme page and other theme pages to come.

Bonus items

Free Resources 1 TikTok Video Saver: SSSTik 2 Instagram Downloader: Snap Insta 3 Youtube Downloader: YTMate) 4 AI Voice Generator: Eleven Labs 5 Auto Captions: SubMagic

Haunt's Site List

Last Updated: June 10, 2023 Alternative search engines Miscellaneous Interesting sites Useful sites Science / math sites Tech sites Privacy / Security...

rentry_co

FREE COURSES
- Copywriting Mini Course
https://mega.nz/folder/o0gUHA4Q#Dxba3Y593YEM3ODbM45HlQ

- Graphic Designing Course
https://drive.google.com/drive/folders/11Abs-oPccVFVDhCqiUMnUC13N2-FxpvF

- Basic to Advanced Dropshipping Course
https://mega.nz/folder/P9slVQqA#qtHKB_DZdJ3rbTWHUExpTg

- Affiliate Marketing Course
https://mega.nz/folder/FxJkia6J#6u7kbN2ud1pSTN4JOwR7YA

- Facts Verse Youtube Automation Course
https://mega.nz/folder/4KJHjKyS#zb19IAg64RtND0GdzOcL7w

Appendix

How to Leverage Email Marketing for Your Digital Products Business

What is Email Marketing?

How I Got Started With Gumroad

open your gumroad store in 3 easy steps

Medium · Feb 16, 2024

The 18 best websites to sell digital products: Ultimate guide [2025] - Checkout Page

Want to know where to sell digital products? We compare the 18 best websites, platforms and marketplaces.

checkoutpage.co · Feb 21, 2024

The HubSpot Blog's 2024 Social Media Marketing Report: Data from 1400+ Global Marketers

We surveyed 1400+ global social media marketers across B2B and B2C industries in the United States to find out what they're investing in this year.

HubSpot · May 13, 2018

How to Find Trending Audio on Instagram

Want to add the latest music to your Instagram Reels and keep up with trends? Here's how you can find trending audio on Instagram.

Guiding Tech · Jun 26, 2024

www.ingramcontent.com/pod-product-compliance
Lightning Source LLC
LaVergne TN
LVHW080102070326
832902LV00014B/2383